AF484982

THE WOMAN AT THE WELL

An Unexpected Conversation

LIVING WATER
COLLECTIVE

The Woman at the Well — An Unexpected Conversation
Written by **Gary A Collings**
Published by **Living Water Collective**.

Contact: LivingWaterCollective2026@gmail.com

ISBN: 9798994988305

Printed in the United States of America.

Also available: An Unexpected Conversation
Going Deeper: A Story-based Study of the Woman at the Well

ISBN: 9798994988312

Before You Begin

This is not a book to rush.

You are not here because you stand at the center of the story,
and not because you are required to arrive at conclusions.

You are here because the same thirst
that drew a woman to a well in Samaria
still draws people toward Jesus today.

Not thirst for water alone,
but for relief,
for mercy,
for a place to lay down what has grown heavy to carry.

As you read, you may recognize yourself in unexpected places.
You may feel resistance, recognition, or quiet longing.

Move slowly.
Pause when something stirs.
You do not need to fix what surfaces.

Just bring it with you.

There is room on this path
for the weight you hold.

"Everyone who drinks this water will thirst again.
But whoever drinks the water I give will never thirst."
John 4:13-14

TABLE OF CONTENTS

PART FIVE

Walking Forward

A Quiet Invitation

Before we begin, take a breath.

There are stories we read,
and there are stories that read *us*.
This is one of the latter.

Not because you stand at the center of it,
and not because you must play a part in history,
but because the same thirst that drew a woman to a well in Samaria
still draws people to Jesus today.

You are here, reading these words,
because somewhere inside you
a jar has begun to feel heavy.

A longing.
A question.
A wound.
A fear.
A story you rarely speak aloud.

Whatever you carry,
whatever you've tucked away in silence,
you do not have to set it down yet.
Just bring it with you.

Walk slowly.
There is room on this path for the weight you hold.

A Note from the Witness at the Well

My name is Mara.

I did not go to the well that day expecting a miracle.
Most miracles come unannounced,
wrapped in the ordinary,
hidden inside moments we nearly walk past.

I went because the air inside my home felt too thin to breathe.
Because grief had its hand around my ribs again.
Because questions I had carried since childhood
had grown too loud to silence.

I went because the well was the one place
where no one asked anything of me.

Perhaps you know that feeling,
the quiet urge to slip away
to the one place where you can be honest
without explaining yourself to anyone.

If so, then come with me.

Stand where I stood.
Feel the heat pressing down on the stones.
Let the wind move the dust around your feet.
Listen for footsteps you aren't expecting.
And allow yourself the possibility
that Jesus might meet you
in a place you didn't plan to be.

Before we begin the story,
there is something you should know:

I am not the woman everyone remembers.
Not the one who spoke boldly,
not the one who ran into the village with news
that startled the whole town awake.

I am simply the one who watched.

The one who lingered in the shade
and heard the sound of living water
spill into the deepest parts of a woman's soul.

And I learned something there,
something I hope you will learn too:

Jesus does not wait for people at their strongest.
He meets them at their thirstiest.

That is why this story has found you.
Not to shame you for what you carry,
but to show you the One who carries you.

So come.
Walk with me to the well.

Bring your jar.
Bring all twelve, if you must.

There is nothing about your story
that will intimidate the One who sits waiting
in the heat of the day.

~ Mara ~

PROLOGUE

Before the Heat of the Day

There are hours in a woman's life that arrive without warning,
quiet thresholds she crosses
not because she is brave,
but because remaining where she is
hurts just a little more than leaving.

That morning, I rose before the sun found the tops of the hills.
Sleep had fled early again,
slipping out the door with the questions I could not answer.
I moved quietly through the house,
careful not to disturb the stillness that grief had stretched thin.

The jar sat near the door,
its familiar weight resting where I had left it the night before.
I told myself I would wait until evening to draw water.
I told myself there was no reason to go early.
But longing has its own voice,
and sorrow has its own schedule.

By midday, I could no longer remain inside.

It wasn't the water I needed.
It was air.
It was space.
It was the one place where my thoughts could breathe
without brushing against the expectations of others.

I had walked that road countless times,
yet that day felt different in a way I could not name.
Do you know that feeling,
when something shifts in the soul,

quietly,
subtly,
as if the ground beneath you is rearranging itself
just enough for you to notice?

The path to Jacob's well wound through dusty fields,
past the fig trees that had long stopped bearing,
past the stones warmed by the relentless sun.
I could hear my sandals scraping against the earth,
a steady rhythm that kept pace with my thoughts.

Regret.
Hope.
Memories that stung.
Dreams that dimmed.
Questions that pressed too hard on the heart.

So many pieces of my story
rested inside the jar I carried.

You may have jars of your own,
ones with names you whisper only to God,
or names you haven't found the courage to speak at all.

Every woman I've ever known
carries something.

Some jars are obvious,
loss, loneliness, longing.

Some are disguised,
competence, busyness, a polished smile.

Some clatter loudly when we walk.
Others ride silently at our side,
waiting for a moment of honesty to reveal themselves.

Mine had become heavier with each passing year.
Yet that day, as I stepped into the heat of the sun,
I sensed, without understanding why,
that the weight I carried
was not the end of my story.

I did not go looking for Jesus.
I did not even know He was near.
I went because the ache inside me
grew too restless to be ignored.

And sometimes,
the road we take to escape our pain
becomes the very path
on which God meets us.

I could not have imagined
how one conversation,
one moment under the blaze of a Samaritan sky,
would begin to loosen the grip
I'd kept on my jar for so long.

But that is where this story begins.
Not with a miracle,
nor with a revelation,
but with a tired woman
walking toward a well
in the heat of the day…

carrying more than she knew
and seen by a Savior
she did not yet recognize.

The Path to the Well

(Walking the Story of John 4)

It was the sixth hour, when the sun stood highest, when I saw Him.

The sun stood high enough to burn the tops of the stones,
and the air shimmered in waves that made even the horizon blur.
Women did not typically walk the road at that hour,
that was the unspoken agreement of our village.

Morning was for gathering water.
Evening was for talk and laughter and shared burdens.
Midday was for no one.

Which is why the well became a refuge for the weary.
For those who needed space to breathe.
For those carrying jars heavier than they could explain.

As I walked, dust gathered at the hem of my robe,
and the familiar ache in my chest
reminded me of the stories I carried but never voiced.

You may carry your own stories the same way.

Some you inherited.
Some were handed to you without warning.
Some grew from wounds you did not deserve.
Some formed from hopes that never came to pass.

But every jar has weight.
And every weight has a reason.

That day, my jar felt heavier than usual.

The path curved.
The well appeared.

And there, sitting where no one expected Him,
was a man whose presence felt like both interruption and invitation.

A Jewish Rabbi.
Alone.
Resting.
Waiting.

The woman with the shattered reputation walked toward Him,
and I, hidden a few steps behind her,
watched a conversation unfold
that would change both of our lives.

And perhaps,
if you listen closely,
it will begin to change yours.

PART ONE
Listening to what we carry

CHAPTER 1

When the Rabbi Asked for Water

I saw Him before He saw me,
a lone figure resting beside the well,
his frame outlined against the heat-hazed sky.

It startled me.

Men did not sit there at midday.
No one did.
The sun was merciless,
and only those avoiding the company of others
walked the road when the shadows disappeared from the stones.

I slowed my steps.
My heart did its familiar flutter,
not fear, exactly,
but the sharp awareness that comes
when your private refuge is no longer empty.

He looked tired.
Dust clung to His feet,
and His robe carried the creases of long travel.
His posture was not threatening,
more weary than imposing,
as if the journey had been heavier than the pack on His shoulders.

Still, I hesitated.

A Jew.
Here.
Alone.

It made no sense.

Jews avoided our region
the way one avoids a wound that hasn't healed.
Our people had a history
that bled too far back for anyone to remember its beginning,
yet close enough that everyone felt its sting.

Why would a Jewish teacher sit at our well?

I considered turning back.
My jar was heavy, but my heart felt heavier.
Sometimes it is easier to remain thirsty
than risk being seen.

But thirst can be stubborn,
and grief even more so.
I stepped closer.

He lifted His head.

And for a moment, just a breath,
I felt as though He was looking *through* me
rather than *at* me.

Not in a way that exposed,
but in a way that recognized.

As if He already knew
the stories I had never spoken.

I dropped my gaze quickly,
hoping He would let me draw water
and slip away unnoticed.

But His voice came,
gentle, steady, surprising.

"Will you give Me a drink?"

The words fell into the silence
like cool water on parched ground.

I froze.

A Jewish rabbi
asking a Samaritan woman
for anything
was unthinkable.

I glanced around,
half expecting someone else to appear,
someone He must be speaking to instead of me.

But there was no one.

Just Him.
Just me.
Just the heat shimmering between us.

"Why do You, a Jew, ask me for a drink?"
The question escaped my lips
before caution could silence it.

He didn't flinch.
He didn't recoil at my boldness.
He didn't look embarrassed or offended.

Instead, He studied me with a softness
I did not know how to receive.

"If you knew the gift of God,"
He said,
"and who it is who asks you for a drink,
you would have asked Him,
and He would have given you living water."

Living water?

I had heard that phrase only in the temple readings,
in stories from our fathers,
in whispered prayers of those who longed for deliverance.

It felt too sacred to belong to ordinary conversation.
Too holy to be spoken
in the dusty heat of midday.

I gripped my jar tighter.

"Sir," I said,
"the well is deep,
and You have nothing to draw with."

My voice sounded steadier than I felt.

I did not know what He meant.
I only knew that something in His tone
reached a part of me I had carefully walled off.

Living water?

It stirred the ache inside me,
the ache I carried silently,

the ache the years had not healed,
the ache I rarely admitted even to God.

He continued to speak,
His eyes never leaving mine.

"Everyone who drinks this water
will thirst again.
But whoever drinks the water I give
will never thirst.
It will become a spring within them,
welling up to eternal life."

Never thirst again?

The words brushed against places in me
I didn't know were still alive.

Longing.
Loss.
The emptiness that followed me
even on my better days.

I swallowed hard.

"Sir… give me this water," I whispered,
before reason could stop me.
"Give me this water so I won't be thirsty
and have to keep coming here."

It wasn't my thirst for water that spoke.
It was the thirst I carried inside,
the one I had never named aloud.

And somehow,
I think He knew that.

He knew the deeper thirst long before I spoke of the lesser one.

He knew the jar I carried
before I ever lifted it.

He knew every private ache
held beneath the surface of my life.

And He did not turn away.

CHAPTER 1 — Reflection

The Thirst Beneath the Surface

When Jesus asked the woman for water,
He was not only speaking to her need,
He was speaking to ours.

The conversation began with thirst
because thirst is something every soul understands.

Some thirsts are obvious:
the longing for companionship,
for healing,
for answers,
for a life that makes sense again.

Others live quietly under the surface:
the ache you carry at night,
the dream you rarely admit,
the hope you have nearly stopped praying for.

Mara saw something in Jesus
before she understood His words:
a recognition,
a gentleness,
a gaze that understood the truth she carried but had not spoken.

Perhaps you felt something stir in yourself
as you read their exchange.

Maybe a familiar ache?
Maybe a forgotten hope?
Maybe the weight of a jar
you've carried longer than you realized?

Jesus began with water
because water reveals the deeper truth:
we are all thirsty for something
no well on earth can satisfy.

The woman asked Him for living water
before she fully understood what it meant.
She simply knew she was tired
of returning to the same place
with the same empty jar
day after day.

You may know that feeling too.

Reflection Questions

1. *As you read Chapter 1, what longing surfaced in your heart, even briefly, that you rarely name out loud?*
2. *Where in your life do you feel the ache of returning to the same "well" without feeling satisfied?*

Notes & Reflections:

Jar #1 — The Jar of Unmet Longing

"The thirst that shapes us."

Long before I understood what Jesus meant by *living water,*
I understood longing.

Not the loud kind people notice,
not the kind that spills into tears or demands to be named,
but the quiet ache that settles beneath the ribs
and becomes part of your breathing.

Some desires burn bright and fade quickly.
Others take root so deeply
that even when you bury them,
they keep growing in the dark.

I carried my longings the way most women do,
hidden, silent, wrapped in strength.

When my mother died,
I longed for her voice.
When my father withdrew into his grief,
I longed to be seen.
When my first marriage ended abruptly,
I longed for something steady enough to trust again.
When my arms remained empty year after year,
I longed for a child's weight against my chest.
When friendships shifted with the seasons,
I longed for a place I could belong without earning it.

Every longing became another drop in the jar I carried.
And over time, the jar grew heavy.

You may have a jar like that too.

Longings you've tucked away:
For healing.
For reconciliation.
For purpose.
For companionship.
For a future you thought you'd have by now.
For the simple reassurance that you matter.

Sometimes we learn to quiet our desires
because disappointment has taught us to expect less.
Sometimes we pretend we don't care
because caring feels too painful.
Sometimes we chase lesser things
because they're easier to reach than the thing we truly want.

But thirst cannot be lied to.
Not for long.

When Jesus spoke of living water,
something in me, something buried and forgotten,
stirred awake.

Hope is frightening when you haven't felt it in years.
Desire is risky when it has cost you tears before.
But His words touched the deepest places in me,
the places I thought were too dry
even for God to notice.

"Give me this water," I said,
not because I understood,
but because I was tired of returning
to the same old emptiness.

I did not realize then
that Jesus was not merely offering me a new source of comfort,
He was offering me Himself.

He does the same for you.

He knows the desires you are afraid to name.
He knows the prayers you whisper only in the dark.
He knows the ache behind the smile you carry in public.
He knows the dreams you have set aside
because they seemed too impossible,
too late,
or too small to matter.

Your unmet longing
is not a sign of failure.
It is an invitation.

An invitation to bring your emptiness to Him.
An invitation to trust Him with the desires you can't fulfill on your
own.
An invitation to let your thirst lead you
not to shame,
but to water.

Some longings will be answered in this life.
Some will not.
But none of them are wasted.
Every desire surrendered to Jesus
becomes a place where His love can reach deeper still.

He is not threatened by your longing.
He is not disappointed by it.
He is not surprised by it.

He meets you inside of it.

That day at the well,
He didn't ask me to pretend I wasn't thirsty.
He asked me to bring Him my thirst.

So I did.
And the water began to rise.

Reflection

What longing have you buried so deeply
that you've nearly convinced yourself it doesn't matter?

What would it look like
to whisper that longing to Jesus
and let Him meet you there?

Notes & Reflections:

CHAPTER 2

When Jesus Asked for the Truth

The air grew still after I asked for the water.

For a moment, I thought the conversation would end there,
that He would offer a kind word,
or let me return to the work of drawing water
and carrying my jar home.

Instead, Jesus looked at me
with a steadiness that felt both gentle and unsettling.

"Go," He said quietly,
"call your husband, and come back."

The words landed softly,
but they reached further than anything He had said so far.

He was not changing the subject.
He was following my thirst to its source.

Thirst always leads somewhere.
And for me, it led to the place
where I had learned who I was.

I hesitated.

"I have no husband," I said at last.

It was true.
And it was not.

I had learned how to speak honestly
without saying everything.

How to offer just enough truth
to remain unseen.

Jesus did not correct me with harshness.
He did not expose me to shame.
He simply named what was already true,
that my life had been shaped by relationships
that could not carry the weight
I had placed upon them.

For the first time,
I realized He was not interested in condemning my past.

He was inviting me to stop hiding from it.

CHAPTER 2 — Reflection

When Jesus Asks for the Truth

When Jesus told her to call her husband, He was not trying to trap her.
He was not shifting from kindness to correction.

He was tracing her thirst to its root.

We often ask God for relief, for living water, for something to change,
and we expect the answer to come as comfort.

But sometimes comfort begins with truth.

Not the kind of truth that humiliates,
but the kind that heals.

Jesus didn't expose her to the village.
He exposed her to herself, gently, steadily,
and then held the moment with mercy.

He didn't reduce her to what she had done.
He didn't label her with her history.
He simply named what was already true,
and in doing so, invited her to stop living divided,
one life on the surface, another life underneath.

That is what Jesus does.

He meets us at the well of what we *think* we need,
and then asks the question that leads us to what we *truly* need.

Not because He wants to shame us,
but because He wants to free us.

Truth is not the enemy of grace.
Truth is often the doorway *into* grace.

Jar #2 — The Jar of Identity

"The thirst to be known, chosen, and held."

For much of my life,
I learned who I was
by who stood beside me.

Who chose me.
Who stayed.
Who left.

Each relationship promised something I needed,
belonging, protection, worth,
a sense of being seen.
And each time that promise faded,
I reached again,
hoping the next one would finally tell me who I was.

Somewhere along the way,
belonging began to replace being known by God.

Relationships became the mirror
through which I tried to understand my own worth.

Identity is a heavy jar to carry
when it is filled by the hands of others.

Jesus does not ask us to deny
our need for connection.
He created us for relationship.

But He knows the difference
between loving others
and letting others define us.

At the well, He told me the truth about my life
without letting that truth become my label.

He did not reduce me to my history.
He did not let my past relationships
name my future.

Instead, He invited me to be known,
fully, honestly, without pretense,
by the One who already saw me.

My identity was never meant to be drawn
from who chose me,
who left me,
or who failed me.

It was meant to flow from the One
who sat waiting at the well
before I ever arrived.

When Jesus asks us for the truth,
it is not to strip us of dignity,
it is to restore it.

Reflection

Where have you learned who you are
from the responses of others?

Whose approval, presence, or absence
has shaped your sense of worth
more than you realized?

What might change if you allowed Jesus,
not your past, not your relationships,
not your failures, to be the One who names you?

Notes & Reflections:

CHAPTER 3

When Worship Becomes a Shield

The truth had barely left His lips
before I felt the familiar urge to retreat.

When Jesus named my life so clearly,
without cruelty,
without surprise,
something in me reached instinctively
for safer ground.

Religion has a way of doing that.

I lifted my eyes from the dust
and searched for a question that might steady me,
something worthy, something respectful,
something that sounded less personal.

"Sir," I said slowly,
"I can see that You are a prophet."

It was easier to speak in titles
than to remain exposed.

"Our fathers worshiped on this mountain,"
I continued,
gesturing toward the rise that stood behind us,
"but you Jews say that the place where people must worship
is in Jerusalem."

The words sounded practiced,
as though I had carried them for years,
ready for the moment when truth pressed too close.

I had learned them well,
the arguments,
the distinctions,
the inherited disagreements
that let us talk *about* God
without having to speak *to* Him.

Jesus did not interrupt me.
He did not dismiss the question
or belittle the history behind it.

But when He spoke,
His voice carried a quiet authority
that did not belong to mountains or temples.

"Woman," He said gently,
"believe Me, the hour is coming
when you will worship the Father
neither on this mountain nor in Jerusalem."

I held my breath.

He was not choosing sides.
He was removing them.

"You worship what you do not know;
we worship what we know,
for salvation is from the Jews.
But the hour is coming, and is now here,
when the true worshipers
will worship the Father in spirit and truth.
For the Father is seeking such people to worship Him."

Seeking.

The word lingered in the air between us.

God was not waiting to be impressed.
He was not measuring correct locations
or tallying proper rituals.

He was seeking hearts.

"God is spirit," Jesus continued,
"and those who worship Him
must worship in spirit and truth."

I had spent years believing worship
was something you *got right*.
A place you went.
A form you followed.
A posture you perfected.

But as He spoke,
I realized how often I had used worship
to manage God,
to keep Him at a respectful distance,
close enough to honor,
far enough to avoid being known.

Religion had given me language,
structure,
and cover.

But it had not given me rest.

Jesus was not stripping worship of meaning.
He was restoring it.

Worship was not about where I stood.
It was about who I stood before.

And suddenly,
the ground beneath my feet
felt far more holy
than any mountain I had ever named.

CHAPTER 3 — Reflection

The Place We Hide in Plain Sight

When the conversation turned toward worship,
the woman did what many of us do
when truth draws too near,
she shifted the focus to religion.

Not because religion is wrong,
but because it can feel safer
than honesty.

Worship, when reduced to form or location,
can become a shield.
A way to speak about God
without opening ourselves to Him.

Jesus did not argue history.
He did not debate tradition.
He gently redirected worship
from *place* to *presence*.

True worship, He said,
flows from spirit and truth,
from a heart that is honest
and a life that is open.

Perhaps you have used worship this way too.

Not as communion,
but as cover.

Not as surrender,
but as structure.

Jesus does not diminish worship.
He deepens it.

He invites us to stop performing
and start abiding.

Jar #3 — The Jar of Religion & Performance

"When doing for God replaces being with God."

I had learned how to speak about God
long before I learned how to sit with Him.

Religion gave me language,
boundaries,
and a sense of belonging.
It taught me what to say,
where to stand,
and how to appear faithful.

But somewhere along the way,
worship became something I offered
instead of someone I met.

Performance is a heavy jar to carry.
It demands consistency,
precision,
and constant self-monitoring.

Am I doing enough?
Am I worshiping correctly?
Am I acceptable here?

Jesus did not ask me to abandon worship.
He asked me to stop hiding behind it.

Spirit and truth
leave no room for pretending.
They invite presence, not polish.

You may carry this jar too.

Perhaps you serve faithfully
but feel strangely distant from God.
Perhaps you know the words of worship
but struggle to rest in His presence.
Perhaps doing has quietly replaced being.

Jesus is not impressed by performance.
He is drawn to honesty.

The Father is seeking worshipers
who will come as they are,
not with rehearsed answers,
but with open hearts.

When worship becomes relationship again,
the jar begins to loosen.

Reflection

Where has worship become something you *do*
rather than someone you meet?

What expectations, spoken or unspoken,
have shaped how you approach God?

What might change
if you allowed worship to be a place of presence
instead of performance?

Notes & Reflections:

CHAPTER 4

When Knowledge Became Control

After He spoke of worship,
of spirit and truth,
of hearts rather than mountains,
I felt the ground steady beneath me again.

Understanding has a way of doing that.

When things become clear,
when ideas fall into place,
we feel momentarily safe.

"I know," I said slowly,
grateful for something familiar to stand on,
"that Messiah is coming.
When He comes,
He will explain everything to us."

It was a statement of faith.
It was also a boundary.

I had learned to wait well.
To trust that answers belonged to the future,
not the present.
To believe that clarity would arrive someday,
just not today,
and not here,
and not in the heat of this moment.

Hope can become a hiding place
when we use it to delay surrender.

I believed in the promises of God.
I just preferred them at a distance.

Jesus did not argue with my expectation.
He did not correct my theology.
He did not send me back to waiting.

Instead, He crossed the final line between us.

"I," He said,
"the One speaking to you,
I am He."

The words were simple.
Unadorned.
Unmistakable.

The Messiah I had placed safely in the future
was suddenly sitting in front of me.

All my careful understanding,
all my patient waiting,
all my quiet control,
fell silent.

I realized then how often knowledge
had given me the illusion of safety.
How believing *about* God
had felt easier than responding *to* Him.

If I knew what was coming,
I could remain unchanged until it arrived.

But Jesus did not come to be explained.
He came to be received.

And in that moment,
the future I had been waiting for
stood before me,
asking not for comprehension,
but for trust.

CHAPTER 4 — Reflection

The Comfort of Knowing, the Risk of Believing

The woman spoke of the Messiah
the way many of us speak of certainty,
as something that will arrive later
and make everything clear.

Knowledge can steady us.
It can organize our faith
and protect us from disappointment.

But when knowledge becomes a substitute for trust,
it quietly becomes control.

Jesus did not leave room for delay.
He did not allow faith to remain theoretical.

He revealed Himself plainly
and invited response immediately.

You may recognize this moment too.

Perhaps you know Scripture well
but hesitate to act on what it asks of you.
Perhaps you trust God's promises
but keep them safely in the future.
Perhaps understanding has replaced obedience.

Jesus does not dismiss knowledge.
He fulfills it.

But He will not be postponed by it.

Jar #4 — The Jar of Knowledge & Control

"When understanding delays surrender."

I believed the right things.
I just believed them in a way
that kept my life unchanged.

Waiting for Messiah
had become a way of managing hope.
A way to keep faith orderly,
predictable,
contained.

Knowledge can feel like control
when it allows us to stay untouched.

But Jesus did not come
to fit neatly into my expectations.
He came to interrupt them.

He did not offer me answers
before offering Himself.

You may carry this jar too.

Perhaps you trust God
but only once you understand the outcome.
Perhaps you delay obedience
until the path feels clear.
Perhaps you believe deeply,
but cautiously.

Control often hides behind wisdom.
But faith begins where certainty ends.

When Jesus names Himself,
He does not wait for readiness.
He invites response.

And sometimes,
the most faithful thing we can do
is stop managing the future
and trust the One standing before us now.

Reflection

Where has understanding become a way
to delay surrender?

What answers are you waiting for
before you are willing to trust?

What might change
if faith meant responding now,
not someday?

Notes & Reflections:

CHAPTER 5

When Being Seen Became Risky

The moment did not last long.

Footsteps approached.
Voices carried on the air.

The ordinary world was returning.

His disciples were coming back from the village,
their arms full,
their conversation easy.
Men who belonged with Him.
Men who would notice me standing there.

And suddenly, everything Jesus had named,
my thirst,
my truth,
my questions,
my hope,
felt dangerously exposed.

I felt the familiar tightening in my chest.
The instinct to step back.
To lower my eyes.
To remember my place.

What would they see
when they looked at me?

A Samaritan.
A woman.
A story whispered too many times
by too many mouths.

I had learned how to live with being seen
without being known.
How to exist under glances
that never asked permission.

But this was different.

Jesus had seen me.
Fully.
And He had not turned away.

Still, fear does not disappear
just because truth has been spoken.

Fear rises when we realize
we can no longer hide.

The disciples looked at me,
then at Him.
I could feel the unasked questions
settling between us.

Why is He speaking with her?
Why here?
Why now?

No one said a word.
But silence can be loud.

I stood there, jar in hand,
feeling the weight of everything I had carried,

not just water,
but history.
Reputation.
Shame I had learned to manage
by staying small.

And then something shifted.

For the first time,
I realized I was more afraid
of returning to my old life
than of standing in the light.

Fear had kept me coming to the well at noon.
Fear had shaped my silence.
Fear had taught me to survive unseen.

But Jesus had not met me
to leave me that way.

I looked down at the jar in my hands.
The same one I had filled and emptied
day after day.
The same one I had clutched
as if it were my only option.

And slowly,
almost without realizing it,
I set it down.

CHAPTER 5 — Reflection

The Fear of Being Fully Seen

Being known is holy.
But it is also frightening.

When Jesus reveals Himself,
He does not expose us to humiliation,
He invites us into freedom.

Still, freedom feels risky
when we have learned to survive through concealment.

The woman did not run because she was fearless.
She moved because something greater than fear
had taken hold of her.

You may recognize this moment.

Perhaps you have felt the pull
to stay quiet
even after truth stirred in your heart.
Perhaps you have sensed God inviting you forward
while fear urged you back.

Fear often whispers
that exposure will cost us everything.

But Jesus reveals truth
so we no longer have to carry it alone.

Jar #5 — The Jar of Fear & Shame

"The fear that tells us it is safer to stay hidden."

Fear is a careful keeper.
It teaches us when to speak
and when to remain silent.
Where we are welcome
and where we are not.

Shame grows best
in places where truth is never spoken aloud.

I had learned to carry my shame
without naming it.
To keep it quiet.
Controlled.
Contained.

But Jesus did not treat my story
as something dangerous.

He treated it as something worth healing.

Fear tells us to hold tighter to the jar,
to keep carrying what we know,
even if it weighs us down.

But healing begins
when we risk being seen.

You may carry this jar too.

Perhaps you fear what others will think
if they know your story.
Perhaps shame has convinced you

that silence is safer than honesty.
Perhaps you have mistaken hiding for wisdom.

Jesus does not shame us into freedom.
He invites us into it.

And sometimes,
the bravest thing we can do
is set the jar down
and step into the light.

Reflection

What fears have shaped where you stay silent?

Where has shame convinced you
that it is safer not to be seen?

What might it look like
to trust Jesus with your story,
even in the presence of others?

Notes & Reflections:

CHAPTER 6

When the Jar Was Left Behind

I did not plan to leave it.

The jar had been part of my life for so long
that I barely noticed its weight anymore.
It had shaped my days,
ordered my movements,
given me a reason to return again and again
to the same place.

But as I stood there,
with the disciples watching
and Jesus still seated beside the well,
the jar no longer felt necessary.

Something else was holding me now.

I looked once more at the vessel in my hands,
the one I had filled,
emptied,
and carried under the heat of countless days.

And I set it down.

Scripture records the moment plainly,
without explanation or emphasis:
She left her water jar and went back to the town.

But nothing about that moment felt small.

Leaving the jar behind
meant leaving the old reasons I came to the well.

It meant releasing the habits that had kept me safe.
It meant trusting that what Jesus offered
would sustain me
even without the thing I thought I needed most.

I did not leave because I had everything figured out.
I left because I had been found.

The jar had once defined my survival.
Now it no longer defined my direction.

I turned toward the path leading back to the village,
the same road I had avoided for years,
the same people I had learned to pass quietly.

This time, I did not walk alone.

A Word Before You Continue

If you're reading this book ahead of a retreat, you may notice the story beginning to feel closer, less observed, more personal.

After the jar is set down, the story no longer stays safely in the past. From here on, it may begin to mirror what we carry ourselves.

This is not something to rush or resolve quickly.

You're welcome to keep reading. Just know that the pages ahead were written to be held slowly, with space for prayer, silence, and shared reflection. There will be time to listen more deeply together.

Read gently.

CHAPTER 6 — Reflection

The Courage to Release What Once Sustained Us

The woman left her jar behind
not because water no longer mattered,
but because it no longer ruled her.

What we carry often begins as provision.
Over time, it can become protection.
And eventually, it can become a prison.

Jesus does not rip the jar from our hands.
He invites us to loosen our grip.

Leaving the jar behind
is not an act of recklessness,
it is an act of trust.

You may be standing at a similar threshold.

Perhaps there is something you rely on
that once helped you survive
but now keeps you from moving forward.
Perhaps a habit,
a role,
a coping strategy,
or a version of yourself
that no longer fits who you are becoming.

Freedom often begins
with a quiet release.

Jar #6 — The Jar of Control & Self-Protection

"What we carry to make sure we are never empty again."

Control feels responsible.
Prepared.
Wise.

It tells us we are simply being careful.

But control can quietly replace trust
when it convinces us
that we must always provide for ourselves.

The jar was never just about water.
It was about certainty.
Predictability.
The comfort of knowing
how the day would unfold.

Jesus did not shame me for carrying it.
He waited until I was ready to set it down.

You may carry this jar too.

Perhaps you hold tightly to routines,
resources,
or identities
that help you feel secure.
Perhaps releasing control feels dangerous
because you've learned not to rely on anyone else.

But Jesus does not ask us
to walk away empty-handed.

He asks us to trust
that what He gives
will be enough.

Sometimes, the clearest sign of faith
is not what we carry forward,
but what we are finally willing to leave behind.

Reflection

What "jar" has helped you survive
but may now be limiting your freedom?

What are you afraid would happen
if you set it down?

What step might Jesus be inviting you to take
once your hands are free?

Notes & Reflections:

CHAPTER 7

When the Story Had to Be Told

I did not rehearse what I would say.

There was no careful plan,
no measured phrasing,
no attempt to make my words acceptable
before they left my mouth.

I only knew I could not keep quiet.

The path back to the village felt different beneath my feet,
shorter somehow,
lighter,
as if the ground itself had shifted
now that my hands were free.

Faces turned as I passed.
Some familiar.
Some guarded.
Some curious enough to slow their steps.

I did not wait for permission.

"Come," I said, my voice rising
before doubt could reclaim it.
"Come and see a man who told me everything I ever did."

The words surprised even me.

Everything.

I did not soften them.
I did not explain them away.
I did not pretend my story was smaller
than it had been.

"Could this be the Messiah?"

The question was honest.
Unfinished.
Still trembling with wonder.

And somehow,
that was enough.

I had spent years believing
that my past disqualified me
from speaking about God.
That credibility belonged to those
with cleaner stories
and steadier lives.

But Jesus had not waited for my perfection
before revealing Himself.

He trusted me with His name
while my hands were still shaking.

People began to move.
Not all at once,
not with certainty,
but with curiosity.

They followed the sound of a changed voice.
They followed the pull of an unfinished story.
They followed hope,
even if they could not yet name it.

And I realized then,
witness was not about having answers.

It was about telling the truth
of what had happened
and inviting others to come and see for themselves.

CHAPTER 7 — Reflection

When Grace Refuses to Stay Private

The woman did not return to the village
with a sermon.
She returned with an invitation.

"Come and see."

Witness begins there.

Not with certainty,
but with honesty.
Not with authority,
but with encounter.

Jesus entrusted His revelation
to someone the village had learned to overlook.

That is how grace moves,
through ordinary people
with unfinished stories.

You may feel unqualified
to speak about what God is doing in your life.
You may worry that your past
makes your voice unreliable.

But God often chooses
those who know thirst well
to point others to water.

Jar #7 — The Jar of Belonging & Witness

"The fear that says our story disqualifies us."

Belonging often feels conditional.
Earned.
Protected by silence.

I had learned to keep my story small
to remain included.

But Jesus did not ask me to edit my life
before speaking His name.

He used the very truth
I once hid
as the bridge back to my community.

You may carry this jar too.

Perhaps you fear being fully known
among the people who know you best.
Perhaps you believe your story
is too messy to be useful.

But witness is not about presenting a finished life.
It is about pointing to a faithful Savior.

Sometimes, the very places we think
disqualify us become the places
God uses most powerfully.

Reflection

What part of your story
have you kept quiet out of fear?

Who might need to hear
not your answers,
but your invitation?

What would it look like
to say, simply,
"Come and see?"

Notes & Reflections:

CHAPTER 8

When Belief Began to Depend on Others

They came out of the village in clusters at first.
A few at a time.
Slow steps.
Careful glances.

I watched from the edge of the road,
my heart beating faster with every familiar face.

Some I recognized immediately.
Others I had learned to avoid.
People who knew my story
before I had learned to tell it myself.

They listened, not to me,
but to the question I had carried back with me.

"Could this be the Messiah?"

It was strange to see them move toward the well
because of words I had spoken.
Stranger still to feel the warmth of attention
settle where isolation had lived for years.

Approval can feel like healing
when you have been invisible for a long time.

As they approached Jesus,
voices overlapped.
Questions spilled out.
Hope rose in the air like dust
caught in the sunlight.

And I felt it,
the quiet pull to measure what was happening
by how many followed,
how many listened,
how many seemed convinced.

Was this what belief looked like now?
Movement? Momentum?
A crowd forming where I once stood alone?

Jesus did not respond to the gathering the way I expected.
He did not grow louder.
He did not step forward to manage the moment.

He remained where He was.

Present.
Unhurried.
Unmoved by the size of the audience.

And I realized then,
belief shaped by others
is fragile.

Crowds can confirm faith.
They can also distort it.

I had spent too much of my life
letting my worth be determined
by how others responded to me.

Jesus was not interested in replacing my isolation
with dependence on approval.

He was inviting all of us,
one by one,
to believe for ourselves.

CHAPTER 8 — Reflection

When Affirmation Feels Like Assurance

The people came because of the woman's testimony,
but they stayed because they encountered Jesus themselves.

That order matters.

Approval can encourage faith,
but it cannot sustain it.

When belief depends on affirmation,
from crowds,
from leaders,
from friends,
it becomes vulnerable to change.

Jesus did not perform for the crowd.
He remained Himself.

You may recognize this tension.

Perhaps you feel strengthened
when others agree with your faith.
Perhaps doubt creeps in
when affirmation fades.

Community matters.
Witness matters.
But faith must take root
in personal encounter.

Jar #8 — The Jar of Approval & Validation

"When belief is measured by response."

Approval is powerful.
It reassures us that we are not alone.
That we are on the right path.

But approval can quietly become a substitute for trust
when we rely on it to confirm what only God can affirm.

I had lived too long
under the weight of other people's opinions
to mistake attention for transformation.

Jesus did not ask me to gather followers.
He asked me to tell the truth.

You may carry this jar too.

Perhaps your faith feels stronger
when others affirm it.
Perhaps you struggle when belief
costs you acceptance.

But Jesus does not anchor truth
to consensus.

He invites each heart
to encounter Him directly.

When approval loosens its grip,
faith grows deeper roots.

Reflection

Where have you looked to others
to confirm what God has already spoken?

How does your faith respond
when affirmation is absent?

What would it look like
to trust Jesus
even if no one else agreed?

Notes & Reflections:

CHAPTER 9

When Faith Became Personal

They stayed longer than I expected.

A day turned into two.
Questions gave way to listening.
Listening gave way to stillness.

I watched from the edges as people gathered,
not around me,
but around Him.

They spoke with Him openly.
Ate where He rested.
Asked what they had carried quietly for years.

And something remarkable happened.

They stopped talking about me.

At first, I noticed it with a strange mix of relief and loss.
My story had been the doorway.
Now it was no longer the center.

When they finally came to me,
their voices carried a new steadiness.

"We no longer believe just because of what you said,"
they told me.
"Now we have heard for ourselves,
and we know that this man really is the Savior of the world."

Not *your* Savior.
Not *our* Samaritan teacher.
The Savior of the world.

Their faith no longer leaned on my words.
And it didn't need to.

For the first time,
I understood that witness is meant to be temporary.

It opens the door,
then steps aside.

Faith that matures
must be encountered,
not inherited.

I did not feel diminished by their words.
I felt free.

My value had not been replaced.
It had been completed.

CHAPTER 9 — Reflection

From Borrowed Belief to Encounter

The people began their journey with curiosity
and continued it with conviction.

They believed first because of testimony.
They believed finally because of encounter.

This is the way faith grows.

Secondhand belief can introduce us to Jesus,
but it cannot sustain us.

At some point,
each heart must respond for itself.

You may recognize this moment too.

Perhaps your faith began through someone else,
a parent,
a pastor,
a friend,
a story that stirred your heart.

But belief becomes personal
when it is no longer dependent
on another's experience.

Jesus invites us all
to hear Him for ourselves.

Jar #9 — The Jar of Comparison & Secondhand Faith

"When belief leans on someone else's encounter."

Comparison quietly shapes faith
when we measure our experience
against the stories of others.

Why doesn't my faith look like theirs?
Why doesn't God speak to me that way?
Why do they seem so certain?

Borrowed belief is not wrong.
It is often where we begin.

But Jesus invites us beyond it.

He does not ask us to replicate another's story.
He asks us to respond to His presence.

You may carry this jar too.

Perhaps you've relied on inherited faith
without knowing how to claim it yourself.
Perhaps comparison has made your journey
feel insufficient.

But faith does not grow by imitation.
It grows by encounter.

When belief becomes personal,
comparison loosens its hold,
and trust finds its own voice.

Reflection

Where has your faith depended
on someone else's experience?

What comparisons have shaped
how you view your own journey?

What might it look like
to listen for Jesus' voice
without measuring it against another's?

Notes & Reflections:

CHAPTER 10

When He Stayed

They asked Him to remain.

Not with urgency.
Not with ceremony.
Simply with honesty.

"Stay with us."

It was a request born not from certainty,
but from recognition,
the quiet knowing that something holy
had entered their ordinary days.

And He did.

Jesus stayed two days among us.

Two days of walking the same paths.
Two days of shared meals and unhurried conversations.
Two days of questions asked without fear
and answers received without force.

I watched how easily He settled among us,
not as a guest to impress,
but as someone who belonged.

For so long, I had believed that encounters with God
were meant to be brief.
Moments to be remembered,
then carried quietly back into real life.

But Jesus was not in a hurry to leave.

His presence did not demand constant attention.
It invited rest.

In those days, something in me softened.
The need to prove,
to explain,
to measure progress,
all of it loosened its grip.

Faith no longer felt like a series of decisions
to be managed carefully.

It felt like companionship.

Jesus stayed not because we had everything right,
but because we were willing to make room.

And I realized then,
sometimes the hardest part of faith
is not believing Jesus will come.

It is trusting Him to stay.

CHAPTER 10 — Reflection

The Courage to Remain

We often imagine faith as movement,
steps taken,
changes made,
progress measured.

But Scripture tells us something quieter here.

Jesus stayed.

Remaining requires trust.
It asks us to release the need
to control outcomes
and simply dwell with God.

You may feel this tension too.

Perhaps you are comfortable with moments of inspiration
but struggle with daily presence.
Perhaps you fear what Jesus might reveal
if He lingers too long.

But God is not impatient with process.

He abides.

Jar #10 — The Jar of Hurry & Restlessness

"When we fear what might surface if God stays."

Hurry convinces us
that faith must always be moving forward.

It leaves little room for listening.
Little space for healing
that unfolds slowly.

I had learned to keep my days full,
movement as protection,
busyness as control.

But Jesus did not rush me.
He remained.

You may carry this jar too.

Perhaps you avoid stillness
because it feels vulnerable.
Perhaps rest feels unproductive
or unsafe.

But transformation does not always arrive
in moments of decision.

Sometimes it comes
through steady presence.

When Jesus stays,
He reshapes us
not by force,
but by faithfulness.

Reflection

Where do you feel pressure
to move faster than your soul is ready?

What might you discover
if you allowed Jesus to linger
in the unfinished places of your life?

How could rest become
an act of trust rather than avoidance?

Notes & Reflections:

CHAPTER 11

When He Left (and the Water Remained)

He did not stay forever.

I knew that, of course.
Travelers come and go.
Teachers move on.
Life resumes its ordinary rhythm.

Still, when the time came,
my chest tightened in a way I did not expect.

Jesus rose early that morning.
There were embraces.
Quiet words.
Promises that felt both complete
and unfinished.

Then He walked away,
down the same road He had arrived on.

For a moment, the old fear stirred.
The familiar ache of absence.
The question that follows every departure:

What happens now?

I had known too many endings.
Too many moments where hope arrived
only to leave again.

But this felt different.

Jesus did not leave emptiness behind Him.
He left fullness.

The well was still there.
The village was still there.
My life was still unfinished.

But the water remained.

Not in the ground,
but within.

I realized then that faith does not depend
on constant proximity.
It rests on transformation.

Jesus had not stayed to make us dependent.
He had stayed long enough
to make us free.

And for the first time,
I did not measure His absence
as loss.

I measured it as trust.

CHAPTER 11 — Reflection

Trusting What Remains

We often fear God's absence
more than we trust His work.

But Scripture shows us something steady here:
Jesus leaves,
and faith remains.

This does not mean grief disappears.
Or questions end.
Or life suddenly becomes simple.

It means we are no longer empty.

You may recognize this season.

Perhaps you once felt God's presence clearly
and now feel the quiet.
Perhaps a season of clarity has passed,
and you are unsure what comes next.

But God does not undo what He has done.

What He begins, He sustains.

Jar #11 — The Jar of Loss & Letting Go

"The fear that says God will leave us empty again."

Loss teaches us to brace for disappointment.
To expect absence.
To hold joy carefully.

I had lived that way for years,
grateful, but guarded.

But Jesus did not ask me
to cling to His presence.

He invited me
to trust His work.

You may carry this jar too.

Perhaps you fear that joy will not last.
Perhaps you hesitate to hope fully
because loss has trained you otherwise.

But the living water Jesus gives
does not evaporate when circumstances change.

It remains.

Sometimes faith is not believing
that God will stay forever beside us.

It is trusting
that He has already done enough
within us to carry us forward.

Reflection

What losses have shaped
how tightly you hold joy?

Where do you fear that God might leave you empty?

What would it look like
to trust that what He has done
will remain—even as seasons change?

Notes & Reflections:

CHAPTER 12

When the Well Became Home

I returned to the well again after He left.

Not because I was empty,
and not because I had forgotten.

I returned because some places
hold memory.

The stones were the same.
The path was familiar.
The air still shimmered beneath the sun.

But I was not the same woman
who had walked there at noon.

The well was no longer a place
I visited in secret.
It was no longer a refuge for avoidance
or a marker of shame.

It had become a reminder.

This was where I had been seen.
Where truth had been spoken gently.
Where living water had found its way
into places I thought were beyond repair.

I realized then that the well itself
was never the point.

It had been a meeting place,
not a destination.

Home was no longer a location.
It was a posture.

To live from the water
meant carrying its quiet confidence
into ordinary days.
Into conversations that were still unfinished.
Into relationships that required patience.
Into a life that would continue to stretch me.

I still drew water.
I still walked the road.
But I no longer carried my jars the same way.

The thirst that once drove me
now guided me.

And I knew this with a certainty
that did not need defending:

Jesus had not changed my circumstances.
He had changed my center.

CHAPTER 12 — Reflection

Living from the Well

The story does not end
with certainty or ease.

It ends with abiding.

The woman did not abandon her life.
She returned to it,
rooted differently.

Living water does not remove us
from the world.
It teaches us how to live within it
without being ruled by thirst.

You may find yourself returning
to familiar places too.

Old patterns.
Old questions.
Old responsibilities.

But returning does not mean retreating
when you return with living water within.

Jar #12 — The Jar of Abiding & Wholeness

"Living from the water, not chasing it."

Wholeness is not the absence of need.
It is the presence of trust.

I no longer measured my life
by what I lacked
or what I hoped would change.

I learned to live from what had been given.

You may still carry jars,
we all do.

But living water changes
how we carry them.

It steadies our steps.
Softens our striving.
Anchors our becoming.

Abiding is not passive.
It is active trust,
returning again and again
to the truth that God has already met us
and will meet us still.

The well did not disappear.
But it no longer defined me.

Final Reflection

What would it look like
to live from the water
rather than chase it?

Where might Jesus be inviting you
to return,
not as you were,
but as someone who has been changed?

What jars can you now carry lightly
because the well has become home?

Notes & Reflections:

Final Word

Living From the Water

The woman did not leave the well with answers to every question.
She left with something better.

She left having been seen.
She left having been known.
She left having tasted a water that did not demand effort, explanation,
or worthiness.

She still had a story.
She still lived in the same village.
She still carried the same history.

But something had shifted.

She no longer lived *from the jar*.

For much of her life, water had been something she carried, managed,
rationed, and returned for again and again.
Living water changed that.

It did not erase her past.
It reoriented her source.

This is the quiet work Jesus does.

He does not remove our jars by force.
He does not shame us for carrying them.
He simply offers another way to live,
not striving for fullness,
but living from what has already been given.

Living from the water does not mean you will never feel thirsty again.
It means thirst no longer gets the final word.

It means you begin to notice when you are reaching for something that cannot sustain you,
and gently return to the One who can.

You may still carry jars.
But they no longer define you.
They no longer direct you.
They no longer decide where you must go to survive.

The well is no longer a place of hiding.
It becomes a place of meeting.

And the water Jesus gives does not rush.
It rises.

Quietly.
Faithfully.
From within.

If You're ready, turn the page. We'll begin on the surface.

A Gentle Invitation Forward

You have walked with a woman to a well.
You have listened as jars were named,
set down,
and re-held differently.

Before you turn the page,
there is no rush.

But if something stirred in you as you read,
a recognition,
a resistance,
a quiet *that sounds like truth*,
you may be wondering
what jars you carry.

The pages that follow are not a test you must pass.
They are an invitation to notice.

You are free to stop at any point.
You are free to answer lightly or honestly.
You are free to skip questions that feel premature.

Jesus never forced truth.
He invited it.

So do we.

You can stop at any time.
You can move slowly.
Jesus is not in a hurry.

PART TWO
Listening to What We Carry

The Surface Test
Noticing What We Reach For

The Surface Test is designed to help you notice
the habits, patterns, and responses
that shape your days.

These questions focus on *what you reach for*
when you are tired, pressured, lonely, or uncertain.

Some answers may feel insignificant.
They are not.

Surface habits often point toward deeper thirsts,
not to shame us,
but to guide us.

Answer honestly, but lightly.
There is no score that defines you here.
This is simply a place to begin listening.

Instructions:
Read each statement slowly and respond honestly.
There are no right or wrong answers.

Before You Turn the Page

You may feel curious to continue.

You may also feel the urge to understand yourself quickly.

Before you go on, pause.

The pages that follow will still be here.
They are not going anywhere.

This test will mean something different
after you have sat with the story
than it will if you rush ahead of it.

If you are reading this book for the first time,
we strongly encourage you to stop here
and return to the test later.

Not because you aren't ready,
but because readiness grows through presence, not speed.

Jesus never hurried truth.
He stayed.

You are allowed to do the same.

Use the following scale:

1 — Not true for me
2 — Occasionally true
3 — Somewhat true
4 — Often true
5 — Very true

Answer lightly. This is a place of noticing, not judgment.

Surface Test Statements (30 total)

Daily Rhythms & Coping

1. I feel uneasy when my day has no clear purpose or plan.
2. I reach for small comforts (food, caffeine, scrolling) when stressed.
3. I stay busy to avoid sitting with difficult thoughts.
4. I feel restless when I am forced to slow down.

Relationships & Approval

5. I feel more secure when others need me.
6. I replay conversations, wondering how I came across.
7. I struggle when I feel misunderstood or overlooked.
8. I feel responsible for keeping relationships running smoothly.

Control & Certainty

9. I feel calmer when I know what's coming next.
10. Uncertainty makes me anxious, even about small things.
11. I prefer having answers over waiting.
12. I feel frustrated when plans change unexpectedly.

Faith & Performance

13. I feel closer to God when I'm doing "well" spiritually.
14. I feel discouraged when my spiritual habits slip.
15. I compare my faith to others more than I'd like to admit.
16. I feel pressure to appear steady, even when I'm not.

Emotions & Inner Life

17. I push through emotions rather than naming them.
18. I minimize my own struggles because others have it worse.
19. I feel uncomfortable admitting weakness.
20. I keep parts of my story private, even from God.

Image & Identity

21. I feel more confident when I'm productive or useful.
22. I struggle when my role or usefulness is unclear.
23. I feel unsettled when I'm not sure who I am in a situation.
24. I feel defined by what I contribute.

Neutral / Uneven Questions (do not score)

25. I enjoy routine more than spontaneity.
26. I find silence either refreshing or uncomfortable.
27. I tend to notice others before noticing myself.
28. I prefer deep conversations over small talk.

Gentle Bridge Questions

29. I sense there may be deeper reasons behind some of my habits.
30. I feel open to exploring what I carry beneath the surface.

If you answered "4" or "5" here, pause before continuing

Surface Test

Scoring & Reflective Guide

Before you look at any numbers, pause.

Take a breath.

This is not a test you pass or fail.
It is a mirror, not to judge you, but to help you notice where your attention and energy most often go.

Step 1 — Do Not Total Everything

You do **not** need to add all your answers together.

Instead, look back through your responses and notice:

- Which statements you marked **4** or **5**
- Which sections seemed to resonate more than others
- Which questions lingered after you read them

Patterns matter more than scores.

Step 2 — Notice Where You Reach

Each section of the Surface Test points toward a different way we try to stay steady:

- Staying busy
- Seeking approval
- Managing uncertainty
- Performing spiritually
- Avoiding emotional exposure
- Defining ourselves by usefulness

None of these are wrong.
They are understandable responses to pressure, fatigue, longing, and fear.

The goal here is not to fix these habits,
only to notice them.

Step 3 — Circle, Don't Analyze

If you find yourself wanting to explain or justify an answer, pause.

Surface awareness does not require explanation.

Simply notice:

- "I do this when I'm tired."
- "I reach for this when I feel uncertain."
- "This feels familiar."

That is enough for now.

Step 4 — Let the Questions Point Gently

Some answers may feel insignificant.
They are not.

Small habits often reveal deeper thirsts, not to shame us, but to guide us.

If a particular statement stirred curiosity, discomfort, or recognition, make a small mark beside it.
You may return to it later, or not at all.

There is no timeline here.

A Gentle Reminder

The Surface Test reveals **what you reach for**, not **why you do it**.

That work comes later, only if you choose to continue.

For now, awareness is enough.

"Jesus never forced truth.
He invited it."

Turn the page when you're ready.

Before the Jars

On the next page, you will see twelve jars.

These jars are not labels.
They are shared human patterns, common places people learn to draw
water when life feels uncertain, painful, or demanding.

You are not required to choose one.
You are not being asked to name yourself.

Simply notice which descriptions feel familiar,
or quietly present.

This surface reflection notices where you reach for water.
The Deeper Test explores why,
but only if and when you choose to continue.

Living Water Collective

The Twelve Jars — Surface Reflection Summary

Awareness is the beginning of invitation.

Jar #1 — Unmet Longing

When "something more" keeps tugging at you
You often feel restless or unsatisfied, even when life is going reasonably well.

Jar #2 — Identity

When roles and relationships shape how you see yourself
You tend to define yourself by what you do, who you're connected to, or how others respond to you.

Jar #3 — Religion & Performance

When faith feels busy instead of restful
You value doing the "right things," but faith can feel more like responsibility than relationship.

Jar #4 — Knowledge & Control

When understanding brings comfort
You prefer clarity, plans, and answers, uncertainty makes you uneasy.

Jar #5 — Fear & Shame

When concerns quietly follow you
You notice recurring worries about the future, safety, or getting things
wrong.

Jar #6 — Control & Self-Protection

When staying guarded feels wise
You tend to manage situations carefully and keep parts of yourself
protected.

Jar #7 — Belonging & Whitness

When inclusion matters deeply
You value being accepted, understood, and part of something
meaningful.

Jar #8 — Approval & Validation

When encouragement fuels you
Affirmation motivates you strongly, and its absence can feel
discouraging.

Jar #9 — Comparison & Secondhand Faith

When you measure your life by others' lives
You notice how others are doing, and sometimes wonder how you
compare.

Jar #10 — Hurry and Restlessness

When staying active feels necessary
You keep moving, scheduling, or doing, slowing down feels
uncomfortable.

Jar #11 — Loss & letting Go

When something didn't turn out as hoped
You carry quiet disappointment or unresolved grief, even if life has
moved on.

Jar #12 — Abiding & Wholeness

When you long for steadiness instead of striving
You desire a faith marked by peace, presence, and trust rather than
effort.

PART THREE

Listening Beneath the Surface

Before You Go Deeper

You may choose to stop here.

Many people do.

The Surface Test alone
is enough for reflection, conversation,
and gentle awareness.

But if you sensed a deeper tug,
if certain questions lingered longer than expected,
you may feel invited to continue.

The pages ahead are more personal.

Please read the next page slowly
before deciding whether to proceed.

A Word of Care

The Deeper Test explores
the *bottom of the jar*,
places shaped by pain, fear, loss, or coping.

Some questions may touch experiences
that feel tender or unresolved.

You are not required to answer everything.
You are not expected to do this alone.

If at any point you feel overwhelmed:

- Pause
- Breathe
- Reach out to a trusted person
- Or bring what surfaced to God in prayer

This is not a diagnostic tool.
It is not a substitute for counseling or care.

Jesus meets us with patience.
So should we.

The Deeper Test

Listening to the Bottom of the Jar

Please read before beginning:

These questions explore places shaped by pain, fear, coping, and survival.
You are not required to answer every question.

Move slowly.
Pause often.
Answer only what you are ready to bring into the light.

Use the same scale as before:

1 — Not true for me
2 — Occasionally true
3 — Somewhat true
4 — Often true
5 — Very true

High scores reflect resonance, not severity.

If a question feels overwhelming, skip it.
Jesus never forced truth. He invited it.

Deeper Test Statements (36 total)

Control & Self-Protection

1. I feel anxious when I cannot control outcomes.
2. I rely on planning or preparation to feel safe.
3. Letting go feels risky, even with God.
4. I struggle to trust when the future feels unclear.

Identity & Worth

5. I feel unsure of my value when I am not needed.
6. I define myself by roles I play or responsibilities I carry.
7. I fear being replaceable or forgotten.
8. I struggle to believe I am loved apart from what I do.

Fear, Shame & Exposure

9. I avoid situations where my weaknesses might be seen.
10. I carry shame about parts of my story I rarely name.
11. I fear how others would see me if they knew everything.
12. I keep emotional distance to protect myself.

Relationships & Attachment

13. I fear abandonment more than I admit.
14. I stay in unhealthy patterns to avoid being alone.
15. I adjust who I am to keep peace in relationships.
16. I struggle to believe others will stay when I'm honest.

Faith, Religion & Performance

17. I feel pressure to appear spiritually steady.
18. I feel guilty when my faith feels weak or quiet.
19. I use spiritual activity to avoid deeper pain.
20. I fear disappointing God.

Comfort, Escape & Coping

21. I turn to habits or substances to numb difficult feelings.
22. I use distraction to avoid emotional discomfort.
23. I struggle to sit with pain without escaping it.
24. I rely on temporary relief rather than lasting healing.

Busyness & Avoidance

25. I stay busy to avoid stillness.
26. Silence makes me uncomfortable.
27. I feel restless when life slows down.
28. I avoid rest because it feels unsafe or unproductive.

Trust & Surrender

29. I find it hard to believe God is enough for me.
30. I struggle to receive rather than earn.
31. I fear what surrender might require of me.
32. I hesitate to bring my full truth to God.

Listening Questions (do not score)

33. I sense God gently drawing my attention to something specific.
34. I feel both resistance and longing as I answer these questions.
35. I recognize patterns that have shaped my survival.
36. I feel invited—not forced—to respond.

Interpreting the Deeper Test

Do **not** total your score.

Instead, notice:

- Which questions stirred emotion
- Which themes repeated
- Which jars feel familiar rather than surprising

These patterns are **not failures**.
They are places where God may already be at work.

If you want clearer direction, the next page helps you summarize.

If you need to pause here, do so.
Scoring can wait.
Truth does not expire.

STEP 1: Transfer Your Scores

After completing the Deeper Test, copy your score for each question into the space below.

Use the same scale you used in the test:
1 = Not at all true
2 = Rarely true
3 = Sometimes true
4 = Often true
5 = Very true

STEP 2: Add Your Jar Scores

For each Jar, **add the numbers** listed next to it.
Write the **total** in the shaded box.

✱ You do not need to average unless you want to. Totals work just fine.

Jar #1 — Unmet Longing

(Questions 21, 22, 23, 24, 33, 34)

21 _____

22 _____

23 _____

24 _____

33 _____

34 _____

TOTAL: _____

Jar #2 — Identity

(Questions 5, 6, 7, 8, 13, 14)

5 _____

6 _____

7 _____

8 _____

13 _____

14 _____

TOTAL: _____

Jar #3 — Religion & Performance

(Questions 17, 18, 19, 20)

17 _____

18 _____

19 _____

20 _____

TOTAL: _____

Jar #4 — Knowledge & Control

(Questions 1, 2, 3, 4, 29, 30)

1 _____

2 _____

3 _____

4 _____

29 _____

30 _____

TOTAL: _____

Jar #5 — Fear & Shame

(Questions 9, 10, 11, 12)

9 _____

10 _____

11 _____

12 _____

TOTAL: _____

Jar #6 — Control & Self-Protection

(Questions 1, 2, 25, 26, 27, 28)

1 _____

2 _____

25 _____

26 _____

27 _____

28 _____

TOTAL: _____

Jar #7 — Belonging & Witness

(Questions 13, 14, 15, 16, 35, 36)

13 _____

14 _____

15 _____

16 _____

35 _____

36 _____

TOTAL: _____

Jar #8 — Approval & Validation

(Questions 5, 6, 17, 18)

5 _____

6 _____

17 _____

18 _____

TOTAL: _____

Jar #9 — Comparison & Secondhand Faith

(Questions 15, 18, 33, 34)

15 ______

18 ______

33 ______

34 ______

TOTAL: ______

Jar #10 — Hurry & Restlessness

(Questions 25, 26, 27, 28)

25 ______

26 ______

27 ______

28 ______

TOTAL: ______

Jar #11 — Loss & Letting Go

(Questions 9, 10, 29, 30, 31, 32)

9 _______

10 _______

29 _______

30 _______

31 _______

32 _______

TOTAL: _______

Jar #12 — Abiding & Wholeness

(Questions 33, 34, 35, 36)

33 _______

34 _______

35 _______

36 _______

TOTAL: _______

Identify Your Primary Jar

- Circle the **highest total**
- That is your **Primary Jar**
- If a second jar is close, note it, many people carry more than one

✳ There is no "best" or "worst" jar.
Each jar simply reveals where Jesus may be inviting you to drink more deeply.

A Jesus Reminder

This test does not tell you who you are.
It reveals where you have been drawing water.

Jesus never shamed the woman for her jar.
He invited her to leave it behind.

Next Step

Turn to the **Jar Reflection Page** that matches your highest score.
Read slowly.
Pray honestly.
And remember:

"The water I give will become a spring within you."

Living Water Collective

The Twelve Jars — A Visual Summary

These jars are not labels.
They are places where thirst has learned to draw water.
Jesus does not shame the jar you carry, He invites you to a better well.

This page reflects where your scores fell, not who you are.

Jar #1 — Unmet Longing

The thirst for something more

What this jar often feels like
A quiet ache that doesn't go away, even when life is going well.
Moments of restlessness, dissatisfaction, or wondering why fulfillment never lasts.
Hope feels risky, yet longing keeps resurfacing.

What Jesus is like here
Jesus does not scold longing, He follows it.
He knows the desires you've learned to manage rather than name.
He offers Himself not as a distraction, but as fulfillment that endures.

Invitation Question
What longing have you stopped bringing to Jesus because you're afraid it won't be answered?

Prayer
Jesus, You see the ache I carry.
I bring You the desires I've tried to quiet or ignore.
Meet me here, not with shame, but with living water. Amen.

Notes & Reflections:

Jar #2 — Identity

The thirst to be known, chosen, and held

What this jar often feels like
Feeling steady when you're needed, and unsettled when you're not.
Defining yourself by roles, relationships, or usefulness.
Wondering who you are when no one is watching.

What Jesus is like here
Jesus sees you apart from what you do or provide.
He names you before others ever could.
Your worth is received, not earned.

Invitation Question
Who, or what, has been naming you instead of Jesus?

Prayer
Jesus, You know me fully and still draw near.
Help me release the identities I've borrowed.
Teach me to rest in who You say I am. Amen.

Notes & Reflections:

Jar #3 — Religion & Performance

When doing for God replaces being with God

What this jar often feels like
Faith that feels busy, heavy, or quietly exhausting.
Serving, showing up, and trying hard, yet feeling distant inside.
Measuring closeness to God by effort.

What Jesus is like here
Jesus does not dismantle worship, He deepens it.
He invites you out of performance and into presence.
God is drawn to honesty, not polish.

Invitation Question
Where has faith become something you manage instead of someone
you meet?

Prayer
Jesus, I'm tired of striving.
Meet me beyond my effort and activity.
Teach me how to be with You again. Amen.

Notes & Reflections:

Jar #4 — Knowledge & Control

The need to understand, manage, or stay ahead

What this jar often feels like
Feeling safest when things make sense.
Anxiety when answers are missing or plans are unclear.
Delaying trust until certainty arrives.

What Jesus is like here
Jesus welcomes questions, but He won't be postponed by them.
He invites trust before full understanding.
Surrender begins where control loosens.

Invitation Question
What answer are you waiting for before trusting Jesus more deeply?

Prayer
Jesus, I bring You my need to understand.
Help me trust You where clarity is absent.
Teach me to lean into You, not certainty. Amen.

Notes & Reflections:

Jar #5 — Fear & Shame

The fear of being exposed or failing

What this jar often feels like
Guarding parts of your story.
Fear of being truly seen or known.
Carrying quiet shame that keeps you small.

What Jesus is like here
Jesus does not expose you to humiliation.
He reveals you to freedom.
He meets you gently, at your pace.

Invitation Question
What fear has been shaping where you stay silent?

Prayer
Jesus, You see what I hide and still love me.
Help me bring what feels unsafe into Your light.
Hold me with mercy and truth. Amen.

Notes & Reflections:

Jar #6 — Control & Self-Protection

Keeping life manageable and contained

What this jar often feels like
Relying on planning, routines, or self-sufficiency to feel safe.
Holding tightly to what once helped you survive.
Fear of what might happen if you loosen your grip.

What Jesus is like here
Jesus does not take the jar from your hands.
He waits patiently until you are ready.
Trust grows slowly, and He honors that.

Invitation Question
What are you afraid would happen if you loosened your grip?

Prayer
Jesus, I've learned how to protect myself.
Help me trust You without fear.
Teach me how to set this jar down, one step at a time. Amen.

Notes & Reflections:

Jar #7 — Belonging & Witness

The desire to be included and understood

What this jar often feels like
Longing to belong without having to perform.
Fear that your story disqualifies you.
Hesitation to speak honestly.

What Jesus is like here
Jesus entrusted His name to someone with an unfinished story.
He uses honesty, not perfection, as invitation.
Belonging grows where truth is spoken gently.

Invitation Question
Who might need your honesty more than your certainty?

Prayer
Jesus, help me trust that my story matters.
Give me courage to speak truth with grace.
Let my life point others toward You. Amen.

Notes & Reflections:

Jar #8 — Approval & Validation

The hunger to be affirmed or appreciated

What this jar often feels like
Feeling encouraged when affirmed, and drained when not.
Measuring faith or worth by others' responses.
Seeking reassurance externally.

What Jesus is like here
Jesus does not anchor truth to applause.
He roots your worth deeper than affirmation.
His voice remains steady when others grow quiet.

Invitation Question
Where have you looked to others to confirm what God has already spoken?

Prayer
Jesus, quiet the voices I chase.
Help me hear Yours more clearly.
Anchor my worth in You alone. Amen.

Notes & Reflections:

Jar #9 — Comparison & Secondhand Faith

Measuring your life by others' stories

What this jar often feels like
Wondering if your faith should look different by now.
Comparing your journey to others'.
Borrowing confidence instead of trusting your own encounter.

What Jesus is like here
Jesus invites you into personal encounter.
He does not ask you to replicate another story.
Faith matures when it becomes your own.

Invitation Question
What would it look like to trust your own encounter with Jesus?

Prayer
Jesus, release me from comparison.
Help me walk my path with You.
Strengthen what You are doing in me. Amen.

Notes & Reflections:

Jar #10 — Hurry & Restlessness

The inability to slow down or rest

What this jar often feels like
Staying busy to avoid stillness.
Rest feeling unproductive, or unsafe.
Always moving, rarely present.

What Jesus is like here
Jesus stayed.
He is not rushed or anxious.
Healing happens in His unhurried presence.

Invitation Question
What might Jesus reveal if you allowed Him to linger?

Prayer
Jesus, slow my spirit.
Help me rest without fear.
Teach me to stay with You. Amen.

Notes & Reflections:

Jar #11 — Loss & Letting Go

Grief, disappointment, or unresolved endings

What this jar often feels like
Guarding joy because loss taught you caution.
Carrying disappointment quietly.
Bracing for what might be taken away.

What Jesus is like here
Jesus leaves, but the water remains.
What He gives is not undone by absence.
He teaches trust beyond proximity.

Invitation Question
Where have you guarded joy out of fear it won't last?

Prayer
Jesus, hold what I have lost.
Help me trust You with joy again.
Teach me to live open, not braced. Amen.

Notes & Reflections:

Jar #12 — Abiding & Wholeness

The invitation to remain, not strive

What this jar often feels like
A quiet readiness.
A desire to live rooted rather than driven.
Not perfection, just peace beginning to form.

What Jesus is like here
Jesus invites you to remain.
Wholeness grows through trust, not effort.
Living water reshapes everything else you carry.

Invitation Question
What would it look like to live from what has already been given?

Prayer
Jesus, teach me to abide.
Help me live from Your grace.
Let Your living water rise within me. Amen.

Notes & Reflections:

PART FIVE

Walking Forward

Couples Use Guide

Living Water Collective — *An Unexpected Conversation*

This story begins with a woman at a well,
but the invitation is for both of you.

Using this book as a couple is not about fixing one another,
comparing answers,
or diagnosing your relationship.

It is about learning to notice your own thirst,
naming what you carry,
and allowing Jesus to meet you there,
together, slowly, and with care.

Before You Begin

- This is **not** a marriage scorecard.
  It is a listening space.
- No one owes full disclosure.
  Share only what feels safe.
- Your spouse is **not** your counselor.
  Be gentle. Be patient. Be kind.

How to Use This Book Well as a Couple

1. Read in parallel, not in debate.
Move through the chapters at the same pace, but resist the urge to
analyze each other's reactions. Let the words settle before you speak.

2. Take the Surface Test separately.
Do not take it together. Do not compare answers.
This protects honesty and reduces defensiveness.

3. Share patterns, not details.
Instead of explanations, try statements like:

- "This jar feels familiar."
- "I noticed I reach for control when I'm tired."
- "That section stayed with me."

You are not required to explain *why*.

4. Do not compare scores.
Comparison turns reflection into competition.
Your goal is awareness, not agreement.

5. Choose one jar at a time.
If different jars surface, that's normal.
You may:

- Focus on one jar per week, alternating whose jar you explore
- Or each work privately while praying for one another

6. Speak in "I" language.
Use:

- "I realized…"
- "I'm noticing…"
- "I felt…"

Avoid:

- "You always…"
- "You should…"
- "This explains why you…"

A Simple Weekly Rhythm (Optional)

- **Day 1:** Read one chapter
- **Day 2:** Reflect privately
- **Day 3:** Share one takeaway each (no fixing)
- **Day 4:** Pray briefly together
- **Day 5:** Rest, do not force progress

If a Moment Feels Tender

Pause.
Breathe.
Hold hands if that feels safe.
Say aloud: *"We don't have to solve this tonight."*

Sometimes the holiest thing a couple can do
is stop
and let Jesus remain in the room.

A Prayer for Couples

Jesus,
You met a woman at a well with mercy and truth.
Meet us the same way.
Teach us to listen without fixing,
to love without pressure,
and to speak without fear.
Help us bring our jars to You, together.
Amen.

Returning to the Well

Closing Blessing

May you leave this story
without hurry.

May the well remain with you,
not as a place you must return to,
but as a reminder
that you have already been met.

May your thirst no longer frighten you,
and may your longings become invitations
rather than burdens.

When old jars feel heavy again,
may you remember the One
who did not ask you to pretend you were not thirsty,
but invited you to bring your thirst to Him.

May you learn to carry truth without shame,
faith without performance,
and hope without control.

May living water rise quietly within you,
steady enough for ordinary days,
deep enough for the nights
when questions return.

And when you walk familiar roads,
may you walk them differently,
not driven by what you lack,
but guided by what you have received.

You are not late.
You are not overlooked.
You are not disqualified by your story.

The One who met a woman at a well
still meets hearts today.

May you rest there.
May you drink deeply.
And may you live from the water
that never runs dry.

Amen.

Appendix A

How the Jars Are Mapped

(For leaders, counselors, and curious readers)

This appendix explains how the Deeper Test questions are mapped to the Twelve Jars. It is provided for those who wish to understand the structure behind the reflection process. The primary text does **not** require this information to be effective.

This material is descriptive, not diagnostic.

How the Method Works (Brief Explanation)

The Twelve Jars framework is designed to identify **where a person tends to draw emotional or spiritual "water"** under pressure, not to label personality, trauma, or spiritual maturity.

Each jar represents:

- a *pattern of coping*
- a *learned place of refuge*
- or a *longing shaped by experience*

The Deeper Test questions are grouped by **themes**, not by pathology. Scores reflect *resonance*, not deficiency.

Overlap between jars is intentional. Human lives are not lived in single categories.

Why Some Questions Map to More Than One Jar

Certain questions appear in more than one jar category. This reflects reality:

- Control often overlaps with busyness
- Identity overlaps with approval
- Fear overlaps with loss
- Longing often hides behind coping

Rather than forcing artificial separation, the framework allows shared influence while still identifying a **primary jar**.

The goal is not precision, it is **recognition**.

Deeper Test → Jar Mapping Overview

Each jar draws from one primary question set, sometimes supported by a secondary set.

(You may include your existing mapping exactly as written here, it is solid and does not need restructuring.)

Important:
A high score does **not** indicate dysfunction.
It indicates a place where God may already be inviting healing, rest, or re-orientation.

Use With Care (Important Note)

This framework is **not**:

- a clinical assessment
- a trauma diagnosis
- a substitute for counseling or pastoral care

Some questions may surface grief, shame, or unresolved experiences. Participants should be encouraged to:

- move slowly
- skip questions when needed
- seek trusted support when emotions feel overwhelming

Leaders should never pressure participants to disclose jar results or personal stories.

Jesus never forced truth.
This framework follows His lead.

Interpreting Results (Pastoral Guidance)

- One primary jar is usually most present
- A secondary jar is common
- Some jars may appear only at certain seasons of life

Jars are **not permanent identities**.
They describe where someone has been drinking, not who they are.

Living water does not eliminate jars.
It teaches us where to return when they grow heavy again.

Appendix B — Leader Facilitation Notes

This page is intended for pastors, facilitators, counselors, and group leaders.

Purpose of This Framework

This material helps people notice where they habitually "draw water," emotionally and spiritually, so they can gently bring those places to Jesus.

This is **not** a diagnostic tool.
It is **not** a counseling curriculum.
It is a **listening aid**.

Leader Posture (Read First)

Your role is not to interpret, fix, or explain results.

Your role is to:

- create safety
- slow the pace
- protect consent
- keep the focus on Jesus, not outcomes

Silence is allowed.
Passing is allowed.
Incomplete answers are allowed.

Use With Care

Participants must always be free to:

- stop
- skip questions
- share at a pattern level only
- withhold personal detail

Never assign a jar.
Never interpret someone else's score.
Never pressure disclosure.

If safety is not present, reflection will not be honest.

When Emotion Surfaces

If someone becomes overwhelmed:

- pause the activity
- normalize stopping
- invite grounding (breathing, stillness, prayer)
- encourage follow-up support if needed

Do not push past resistance.
Jesus never forced truth. He invited it.

A Final Reminder for Leaders

The goal is not to empty jars.
The goal is to notice where people go for water,
and gently return attention to Christ as the source.

Jars are indicators, not identities.
Transformation is never rushed.

Living water rises quietly.

Notes & Reflections:

Notes & Reflection: